T0070023

REAL **mvp**kids

I Can Wash My Hands™

SOPHIA DAY®

Written by Celestte Dills   *Illustrated by* Timothy Zowada

The Sophia Day® Creative Team-

Celestte Dills, Timothy Zowada, Stephanie Strouse,
Megan Johnson, Kayla Pearson, Patty Lopez Gregersen, Mel Sauder

A **special thank you** to our reviewers who graciously give us
feedback, edits, and help ensure that our products remain accurate,
applicable, and genuinely diverse.

Text and pictures copyrighted © 2021 by MVP Kids Media, LLC
All rights reserved. No part of this publication may be reproduced
in whole or in part by any mechanical, photographic or electronic
process, or in the form of any audio or video recording nor may
it be stored in a retrieval system or transmitted in any form or by
any means now known or hereafter invented or otherwise copied
for public or private use without the written permission of
MVP Kids Media, LLC.

Published and Distributed by MVP Kids Media, LLC -
Mesa, Arizona, USA
Printed in China

Designed by Stephanie Strouse

ISBN 978-1-64999-986-3
DOM Mar 2021
Job # 17-002-01

May your childhood be filled with adventure, your days with hope and your learnings with wisdom, and may you continuously grow as an MVP Kid, preparing to lead a responsible, meaningful life.

- SOPHIA DAY

Hello! I'm Aanya . . .

and this is my pet cat, Neela.

Neela loves
to be petted.

Sometimes,
Neela's fur gets
on my hands.

I can wash my hands to get them clean.

4

When I was younger, I didn't know how or when to wash my hands.

But, with practice, I learned how and when to wash my hands.

I wet my hands.

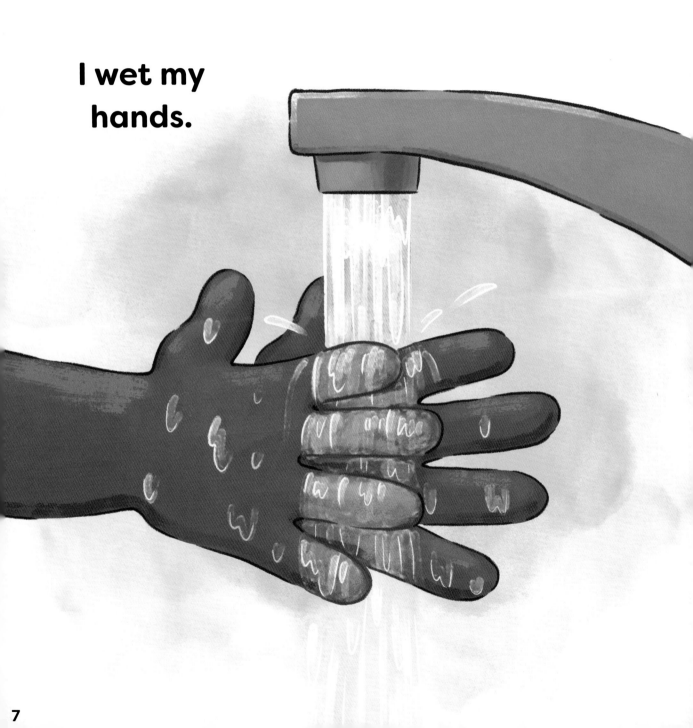

I use soap to scrub my
hands for 20 seconds.
That's long enough to sing
The ABC Song!

I rinse my hands.

I dry my hands.

Before I help with cooking and when I am ready to eat...

I can wash
my hands.

After I cough, sneeze, or use the bathroom . . .

ACHOO!

I can wash
my hands.

14

Whenever my hands get sticky or dirty . . .

I can wash
my hands.

16

I wash my hands . . .

to be
safe and
healthy!

I can wash my hands!

1. Wet my hands.

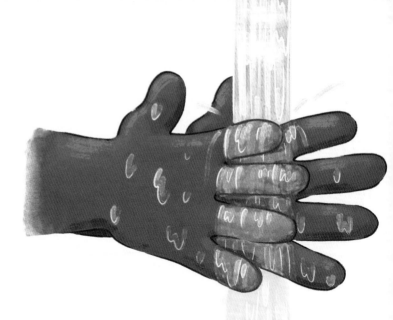

2. Use soap and scrub for 20 seconds.

3. Rinse my hands.

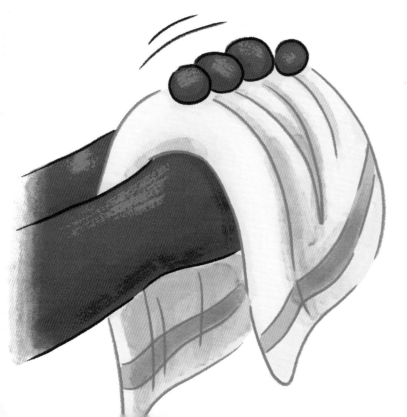

4. Dry my hands.

meet our

mvpkids®

featured in
I Can Wash My Hands

Hi! My name is Aanya Patel.
I love to work on puzzles and play with my pet cat, Neela. My cochlear implants help me hear. Our family learned to communicate with American Sign Language! In this story, I learned how and when to clean my hands!

Also featuring...

Mr. Pasha Patel
Father

Mrs. Myra Patel
Mother

Neela
Pet Cat

Frankie Russo
MVP Kid

HELPFUL TEACHING TIPS
I Can Wash My Hands

According to the Centers for Disease Control and Prevention, handwashing can prevent one in three digestive tract illnesses and one in five respiratory infections like the cold and flu! Handwashing is one of the most effective, easiest, and least expensive ways to keep everyone healthy.

Handwashing Steps

Steps to wash your hands:
1. Wet hands.
2. Use soap and scrub hands for 20 seconds.
3. Rinse hands.
4. Dry hands.

Make a copy of pages 19-20 and display the handwashing steps at children's eye level near sinks.

Scrub for 20 Seconds

You can help children scrub for 20 seconds by using a timer or singing the following song twice:

"Wash, Wash, Wash My Hands"
(to the tune of "Row, Row, Row Your Boat")

Wash, wash, wash my hands,
Play this washing game.
Rub and scrub, and scrub and rub.
The germs go down the drain.

I Can:

- Wet my hands.
- Use soap and scrub my hands for 20 seconds.
- Rinse my hands.
- Dry my hands.

Germs Spread!

Show children how germs spread and explain the importance of handwashing. Fill a clean spray bottle with water. Demonstrate germs by spraying water on your children's hands.

Ask children to touch surfaces or objects and observe how the water droplets transfer. Count how many items become wet before their hands become dry.

Go Away Germs!

Show children how soap can chase away germs. Sprinkle a few pinches of pepper (to represent germs) into a small water filled bowl.

Have your child dip one finger into liquid soap and then into the water. The pepper will scatter away from the soap-covered finger.

*Check out our MVP Kids Emotion Cards and Solve It! Cards, and view additional tip and reference information at **www.MVPKids.com**.*

29

Grow up with our **mvp**kids

CELEBRATE!™
Board Books
Ages 0-6

Our **CELEBRATE!™** board books for toddlers and preschoolers focus on social, emotional, educational, and physical needs. Helpful Teaching Tips are included in each book to equip parents to guide their children deeper into the subject of each book.

Celebrate!™
Paperbacks
Ages 4-8

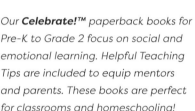

Our **Celebrate!™** paperback books for Pre-K to Grade 2 focus on social and emotional learning. Helpful Teaching Tips are included to equip mentors and parents. These books are perfect for classrooms and homeschooling!

I Can Be an MVP!™
Ages 2-6

The **I Can Be an MVP™** paperback series helps children ages 2-6 practice social and emotional skills and self-help routines. These short stories are designed with simple, memorable scripts and illustrations focusing on a singular behavior or process.

Playful Apprentice™
Ages 4-8

The **Playful Apprentice™** series is an imaginative view into children's role-playing. These picture books show a variety of community roles and career options that fuel dreams and support character building. Readers will be inspired by interviews and advice from real professionals!

*Our **Mighty Tokens™** learn-to-read series helps emerging readers learn positive concepts with an experienced reader. Each book deposits tokens of affirmation into children so that they may someday become mighty adults.*

Ages 4-8

Early Elementary

Ages 4-10

*Our **Help Me Become™** series for early elementary readers tells three short stories of our MVP Kids® inspiring character growth. Each story concludes with a discussion guide to help your child process the story and apply the concepts.*

Elementary

Ages 6-12

*Our **Help Me Understand™** series for elementary readers shares the stories of our MVP Kids® learning to understand and manage a specific emotion. Readers will gain tools to take responsibility for their own emotions and develop healthy coping skills.*

DNA CHRONICLES™

Ages 8 and up

*Step back in time with **DNA Chronicles™**, our historical fiction adventure series. Our MVP Kids® weave together the past and the present, reliving actual historical events to experience the history and culture of their ancestors. In these chapter books, readers will learn about the desire and fortitude it takes to commit to life's most important values, life skills, and accomplishments.*

Inspire character with our growing line of products, including books, puppets, classroom and home SEL programs, music, apps, and more! **Visit www.MVPKids.com for more information.**

SOPHIA DAY'S®

instill® SEL

In English y Español

Instill Character®

SOCIAL AND EMOTIONAL LEARNING CLASSROOM PROGRAM (AGES 2-6)

Sophia Day's Instill SEL classroom activities teach through music, creative art, movement, puppets, and pretend play to create strong habits that form long-term thought patterns, attitudes, and actions.

Instill SEL is built on CASEL's Five Core Competencies, making it easily integrated into your current comprehensive curriculum.

We value safety.

Valoramos la seguridad.

We can be safe.

Podemos estar a salvo.

Valoramos a los demás.

Our classroom program is available in English or Spanish with bilingual tools!

SOPHIA DAY'S®
instill® SEL
AT HOME

SOCIAL AND EMOTIONAL LEARNING TOOLKIT FOR YOUR HOME (AGES 2-6)

This simple and effective program provides families with tools and strategies to support:

- Decreased frustration
- Less challenging behavior
- Better communication
- Stronger relationships

by increasing emotional understanding, practicing problem-solving skills, developing healthy habits, and strengthening social skills.

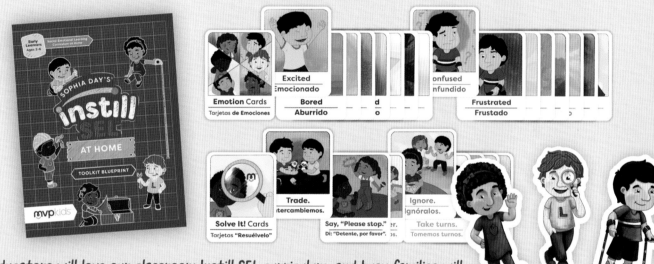

Educators will love our classroom Instill SEL curriculum, and busy families will thrive from our fun and easy-to-use tools in our Instill SEL at Home!

INTERESTED IN THE POSSIBILITIES OF SOCIAL AND EMOTIONAL LEARNING WITH MVP KIDS IN YOUR CLASSROOM OR HOME?

Learn more about both of our programs, Sophia Day's Instill SEL and Instill SEL at Home, on our website, www.MVPKidsED.com.

Yong Chen

Leo Russo

Frankie Russo

Julia Rojas

Aanya Patel

Annie James

Blake James

Sarah Cohen-Goldstein